MONEY

ANDREW MURRAY

SANAGE
PUBLISHING HOUSE

Paperback: 978-939089658-5

Sanage Publishing House LLP
Mumbai, India

sanagepublishing@gmail.com

Andrew Murray (9 May 1828 – 18 January 1917) was a South African writer, teacher and Christian pastor. After receiving his education in Scotland and Holland, he returned to South Africa and spent many years there as both a pastor and missionary. He wrote over two hundred books, including some of the most enduring classics of Christian literature.

CONTENTS

I. CHRIST'S ESTIMATE OF MONEY

.$.

"Jesus beheld how the people cast money into the treasury: and many that were rich cast in much. And a certain poor widow came, and cast in a farthing. Jesus called His disciples, and saith unto them, This poor widow hath cast more in than all: for all they did cast in of their abundance; but she of her want did cast in all that she had, even all her living."--_Mark_ xii. 41.

In all our religion and our Bible study, it is of the greatest consequence to find out what the mind of Christ is, to think as He thought, and to feel just as He felt. There is not a question that concerns us, not a single matter that ever comes before us, but we find in the words of Christ something for our guidance and help. We want to-day to get at the mind of Christ about Money; to know exactly what He thought, and then to think and act just as He would do. This is not an easy thing. We are so under the influence of the world around us, that the fear of becoming utterly unpractical if we thought and acted just like Christ, easily comes upon us. Let us not be afraid; if we really desire to find out what is His mind, He will guide us to what He wants us to think and do. Only be honest in the thought: I want to have Christ teach me how to possess and how to use my money.

Look at Him for a moment sitting here over against the treasury, watching the people putting in their gifts. Thinking about money in the church, looking after the collection: we often connect that with Judas, or some hard-worked deacon, or the treasurer or collector of some society. But see here--Jesus sits and watches the collection. And as He does it, He weighs each gift in the balance of God, and puts its value on it. In heaven He does this still. Not a gift for any part of God's work, great or small, but He notices it, and puts its value on it for the blessing, if any, that it is to bring in time or eternity. And He is willing, even here on earth in the waiting heart, to let us know what He thinks of our giving. Giving money is a part of our religious life, is watched over by Christ, and must be regulated by His word. Let us try and discover what the scriptures have to teach us.

1. Money giving a sure test of character.

In the world money is the standard of value. It is difficult to express all that money means. It is the symbol of labor and enterprise and cleverness. It is often the token of God's blessing on diligent effort. It is the equivalent of all that it can procure of the service of mind or body, of property or comfort or luxury, of influence and power. No wonder that the world loves it, seeks it above everything, and often worships it. No wonder that it is the standard of value not only for material things, but for man himself, and that a man is too often valued according to his money.

It is, however, not only thus in the kingdom of this world, but in the kingdom of heaven too, that a man is judged by his money, and yet on a different principle. The world asks, _what_ does a man own? Christ, _how_ does he use it? The world thinks more about the money getting; Christ about the money giving. And when a man gives, the world still asks, _what_ does he give? Christ asks, how does he give? The world looks at the money and its amount, Christ at the man and his motive. See this in the story of the poor widow. Many that were rich cast in _much_; but it was _out of their abundance;_ there was no real sacrifice in it; their life was as full and comfortable as ever, it cost them nothing. There was no special love or devotion to God in it; part of an easy and traditional religion. The widow cast in _a farthing_. Out of her want she cast in all that she had, even all her living. She gave all to God without reserve, without holding back anything, she gave all.

How different our standard and Christ's. We ask how much a man _gives_. Christ asks, how much he _keeps_. We look at the gift. Christ asks whether the gift was a sacrifice. The widow kept nothing over, she gave all; the gift won His heart and approval, for it was in the spirit of His own self-sacrifice, who, being rich, became poor for our own sakes. They--out of their abundance--cast in much: She, out of her want--all that she had.

But if our Lord wanted us to do as she did, why did He not leave a clear command? How gladly then would we do it. Ah! there you have it. You want a command to make you do it: that would just be the spirit of the world in the church looking at _what_ we give, at our giving all. And that is just what Christ does not wish and will not have. He wants the generous love that does it unbidden. He wants every gift to be a gift warm and bright with love, a true free will offering. If you want the Master's approval as the poor widow had it, remember one thing: you must put all at His feet, hold all at His disposal. And that, as the spontaneous expression of a love that, like Mary's, cannot help giving, just because it loves.

All my money giving--what a test of character! Lord Jesus! Oh give me grace to love Thee intently, that I may know how to give.

2. Money giving a great means of grace.

Christ called His disciples to come and listen while He talked to them about the giving He saw there. It was to guide their giving and ours. Our giving, if we listen to Christ with the real desire to learn, will have more influence on our growth in grace than we know.

The spirit of the world, "the lust of the flesh, the lust of the eye, and the pride of life." Money is the great means the world has for gratifying its desires. Christ has said of His people, "they are not of the world, as I am not of the world." They are to show in their disposal of money that they act on unworldly principle, that the spirit of heaven teaches them how to use it. And what does that spirit suggest? Use it for spiritual purposes, for what will last for eternity, for what is pleasing to God. "They that are Christ's have crucified the flesh and its lusts." One of the ways of manifesting and maintaining the crucifixion of the flesh is never to use money to gratify it. And the way to conquer every temptation to do so, is to have the heart filled with large thoughts of the spiritual power of money. Would you learn to keep the flesh crucified--refuse to spend a penny on its gratification. As much as money spent on self, may nourish and strengthen and comfort self, money sacrificed to God may help the soul in the victory that overcometh the world and the flesh.

Our whole life of faith may be strengthened by the way we deal with money. Many men have to be engaged continually in making money--by nature the heart is dragged down and bound to earth in dealing with what is the very life of the world. It is faith that can give a continual victory over this temptation. Every thought of the danger of money, every effort to resist it, every loving gift to God, helps our life of faith. We look at things in the very light of God. We judge of them as out of eternity, and the money passing through our hands and devoted to God may be a daily education in faith and heavenly-mindedness.

Very specially may our money giving strengthen our life of love. Every grace needs to be exercised if it is to grow; most of all is this true of love. And--did we but know it--how our money might develop and strengthen our love, as it called us to the careful and sympathizing consideration of the needs of those around us. Every call for money, and every response we give, might be the stirring of a new love, and the aid to a fuller surrender to its blessed claims.

Money giving may be one of your choicest means of grace, a continuous fellowship with God in the renewal of your surrender of your all to Him, and in proof of the earnestness of your heart to walk before Him in self-denial, and faith and love.

3. Money giving a wonderful power for God.

What a wonderful religion Christianity is. It takes money, the very embodiment of the power of sense of this world, with its self-interest, its covetousness, and its pride, and it changes it into an instrument for God's service and glory.

Think of the poor. What help and happiness is brought to tens of thousands of helpless ones by the timely gift of a little money from the hand of love. God has allowed the difference of rich and poor for this very purpose--that just as in the interchange of buying and selling mutual dependence upon each other is maintained among men--so in the giving and receiving of charity there should be abundant scope for the blessedness of doing and receiving good. He said, "It is more blessed to give than to receive." What a Godlike privilege and blessedness to have the power of relieving the needy and making glad the heart of the poor by gold or silver! What a blessed religion that makes the money we give away a source of greater pleasure than that which we spend on ourselves! The latter is mostly spent on what is temporal and carnal, that spent in the work of love has eternal value, and brings double happiness, to ourselves and others.

Think of the church and its work in this world; of missions at home and abroad, and the thousand agencies for winning men from sin to God and Holiness. Is it indeed true that the coin of this world, by being cast into God's treasury in the right spirit, can receive the stamp of the mint of heaven, and be accepted in exchange for heavenly blessings? It is true. The gifts of faith and love go not only into the Church's treasury, but into God's own treasury, and are paid out again in heavenly goods. And that not according to the earthly standard of value, where the question always is, How much? but according to the standard of heaven, where men's judgments of much and little, great and small, are all unknown.

Christ has immortalized a poor widow's farthing. With His approval it shines through the ages brighter than the brightest gold. It has been a blessing to tens of thousands in the lesson it has taught. It tells you that your farthing, if it be your all, that your gift, if it be honestly given (as you all ought to give to the Lord), has His approval, His stamp, His eternal blessing.

If we did but take more time in quiet thoughtfulness for the Holy Spirit to show us our Lord Jesus in charge of the Heavenly Mint, stamping every true gift, and then using it for the Kingdom, surely our money would begin to shine with a new lustre. And we should begin to say--The less I can spend on myself, and the more on my Lord, the richer I am. And we shall see how, as the widow was richer in her gift and her grace than the many rich, so he is richest who truly gives all he can.

4. Money giving a continual help on the ladder to heaven.

You know how often our Lord Jesus spake of this in His parables.

In that of the unjust steward He said, Make friends of the Mammon of unrighteousness, that they may receive you in the eternal habitations. In the parable of the talents He said, "Thou oughtest to have put _my money_." The man who had not used his talent, lost all. In the parable of the sheep and the goats, it is they who have cared for the needy and the wretched in His name, who shall hear the word--Come, ye blessed of my Father.

We cannot purchase heaven--as little with money as with works. But in your money giving, heavenly-mindedness and love to Christ, and love to men, and devotion to God's work, are cultivated and proved. The "Come, ye blessed of My Father, inherit the Kingdom," will take count of the money truly spent on Christ and his work. Our money giving must prepare us for heaven.

Oh! how many there are who if heaven and holiness could be bought for a thousand pounds would give it. No money can buy those. But if they only knew, money can wondrously help on the path of holiness and heaven. Money given in the spirit of self-sacrifice, and love, and faith in Him who has paid all, brings a rich and eternal reward. Day by day give as God blesses and as He asks--it will help to bring heaven nearer to you, it will help to bring _you_ nearer to heaven.

The Christ who sat over against the treasury is my Christ. He watches my gifts. What is given in the spirit of whole-hearted devotion and love He accepts. He teaches His disciples to judge as He judges. He will teach me how to give--how much, how lovingly, how truthfully.

Money--this is what I want to learn from Him above all--money, the cause of so much temptation and sin, and sorrow and eternal loss; money, as it is received and administered and distributed at the feet of Jesus, the Lord of the Treasury, becomes one of God's choicest channels of grace to myself and to others. In this, too, we are more than conquerors through Him who loved us.

Lord! give Thy Church, in her poverty, give us all, the spirit of the poor widow.

☩☩☩

II. THE HOLY SPIRIT AND MONEY

.$.

When the Holy Spirit came down at Pentecost to dwell in men, He assumed the charge and control of their whole life. They were to be or do nothing that was not under His inspiration and leading. In everything they were to move and live and have their being "in the Spirit," to be wholly spiritual men. Hence it followed as a necessity that their possessions and property, that their money and its appropriations were subjected to His rule too, and that their income and expenditure were animated by new and hitherto unknown principles. In the opening chapters of the Acts we find more than one proof of the all-embracing claim of the Holy Spirit to guide and judge in the disposal of money. If I want as a Christian to know how to give, let me learn here what the teaching of the Holy Spirit is as regards the place money is to have in my Christian life and in that of the Church.

First we have: _The Holy Spirit taking possession of the money_.

"All that believed were together, and had all things common; and they sold their possessions and goods, and parted them to all according as every man had need."--Acts ii. 44, 45. And again, Acts iv. 34: "As many as were possessors of land or houses, sold them, and brought the prices of the things that were sold, and laid them at the Apostles' feet. And Barnabas having a field, sold it, and brought the money and laid it at the Apostles' feet." Without any command or instruction, in the joy of the Holy Spirit, the joy of the love which He had shed abroad in their heart, the joy of the heavenly treasures that now made them rich, they spontaneously parted with their possessions and placed them at the disposal of the Lord and His servants.

It would have been strange had it been otherwise, and a terrible loss to the Church. Money is the great symbol of the power of happiness of this world; one of its chief idols, drawing men away from God; a never-ceasing temptation to worldliness, to which the Christian is daily exposed. It would not have been a full salvation that did not provide complete deliverance from the power of money. The story of Pentecost assures us that when the Holy Spirit comes in His fulness into the heart, then earthly possessions lose their place in it, and money is only valued as a means of proving our love and doing service to our Lord and our fellow men. The fire from heaven that finds a man upon the altar and consumes the sacrifice, finds his money too, and makes it all ALTAR GOLD, holy to the Lord.

We learn here the true secret of Christian giving, the secret, in fact, of all true Christian living--the joy of the Holy Ghost. How much of our giving then has there been in which this element has been too much lacking. Habit, example, human argument and motive, the thought of duty, or the feeling of the need around us, have had more to do with our charities than the power and love of the Spirit. It is not that what has just been mentioned is not needful. The Holy Spirit makes use of all these elements of our nature in stirring us to give. There is a great need for inculcating principles and fixed habits in regard to giving. But what we need to realize is that all this is but the human side, and cannot suffice if we are to give in such measure and spirit as to make every gift a sweet-smelling sacrifice to God and a blessing to our own souls. The secret of true giving is the joy of the Holy Ghost.

The complaint in the Church as to the terrible need of more money for God's work, as to the terrible disproportion between what God's people spend on themselves and devote to their God, is universal. The pleading cry of many of God's servants who labor for the poor and the lost, is often heart-piercing. Let us take to heart the solemn lesson: this is simply a proof of the limited measure in which the power of the Holy Spirit is known among believers. Let us for ourselves pray most fervently, that our whole life may be so lived in the joy of the Holy Spirit, a life so absolutely yielded to Him and His rule, that all our giving may be a spiritual sacrifice, through Jesus Christ.

Our second Pentecostal lesson on money we find in Acts iii. 6: "Then Peter said, silver and gold have I none, but what I have that give I thee. In the name of Jesus Christ of Nazareth, walk!" Here it is: _The Holy Spirit dispensing with money_.

Our first lesson was: The Church of Pentecost needs money for its work; the Spirit of Pentecost provides money; money may be at once a sure proof of the Spirit's mighty working, and a blessed means of opening the way for His fuller action.

But there is a danger ever near. Men begin to think that money is the great need; that abundance of money coming in is a proof of the Spirit's presence; that money must be strength and blessing. Our second lesson dissipates these illusions, and teaches us how the power of the Spirit can be shown where there is no money. The Holy Spirit is the mighty power of God, now condescending to use the money of His saints, then again proving how divinely independent He is of it. The Church must yield herself to be guided into this double truth; the Holy Spirit claims all its money; the Holy Spirit's mightiest works may be wrought without it. The Church must never beg for money as if this were the secret of her strength.

See these Apostles, Peter and John, penniless in their earthly poverty, and yet by virtue of their poverty, mighty to dispense heavenly blessings. "Poor, yet making many rich." Where had they learned this? Peter says, "Silver and gold have I none; in the name of Jesus Christ, walk." It points us back to the poverty which Christ had enjoined upon them, and of which He had set them the wonderful example. By his holy poverty He would prove to men what a life of perfect trust in the Father, is how the possession of heavenly riches makes independent of earthly goods, how earthly poverty fits the better for holding and for dispensing eternal treasures. The inner circle of His disciples found in following the footsteps of His poverty the fellowship of His power. The Apostle Paul was taught by the Holy Spirit the same lesson. To be ever in external things, utterly loose even from earth's lawful things, is a wonderful, he almost appears to say, an indispensable help in witnessing to the absolute reality and sufficiency of the unseen heavenly riches.

We may be sure that as the Holy Spirit begins to work in power in His Church, there will again be seen His mighty operation in the possession of His people. Some will again by their giving make themselves poor, in the living faith of the incomprehensible worth of their heavenly heritage, and the fervent joy the Spirit gives them in it. And some who are poor and in great straits with their work for God will learn to cultivate more fully the joyful consciousness: "Silver and gold have I none: what I have I give: in the name of Jesus Christ, walk." And some who are not called to give all, will yet give with an unknown liberality, because they begin to see the privilege of giving all, and long to come as near as they can. And we shall have a Church, giving willingly and abundantly, and yet not for a moment trusting in its money, but honoring those most who have the grace and the strength to be followers of Jesus Christ in His poverty.

Our third lesson is: _The Holy Spirit testing the money_. All the money that is given, even in a time when the Holy Spirit is moving mightily, is not given under His inspiration. But it is all given under His holy supervision, and He will from time to time, to each heart that honestly yields to Him, reveal what there may be wanting or wrong. Listen: "Barnabas having a field, sold it, and brought the money. _But_ Ananias sold a possession and kept back part of the price, and brought a certain part, and laid it at the Apostles' feet." Ananias brought his gift, and with his wife was smitten dead. What can have made the gift such a crime? He was a deceitful giver. He kept back part of the price. He professed to give all, and did not. He gave with half a heart and unwillingly, and yet would have the credit of having given all. In the Pentecostal Church the Holy Ghost was the author of the giving: his sin was against the Holy Ghost. No wonder that it is twice written: "great fear came upon the whole Church, and upon all who heard it." If it is so easy to sin even in giving, if the Holy Spirit watches and judges all our giving, we may well beware and fear.

And what was the sin? Simply this: he did not give all he professed. This sin, not in its greatest form, but in its spirit and more subtle manifestations, is far more common than we think. Are there not many who say they have given their all to God, and yet prove false to it in the use of their money? Are there not many who say all their money is their Lord's, and that they hold it as His stewards, to dispose of it as He directs, and yet who, in the amount they spend on God's work, as compared with that on themselves, and in accumulating for the future, prove that Stewardship is but another name for ownership.

Without being exactly guilty of the sin of Judas, or Caiaphas, or Pilate in crucifying our Lord, a believer may yet partake with them in the spirit in which he acts. Even so we may be grieving the Holy Ghost, even while we condemn the sin of Ananias, by giving way to the spirit in which he acted, and withholding from God what we have professed to give Him. Nothing can save us from this danger, but the holy fear of ourselves, the very full and honest surrender of all our opinions, and arguments, about how much we may possess, and how much we may give, to the testing and searching of the Holy Spirit. Our giving must be in the light, if it is to be in the joy of the Holy Ghost.

And what was it that led Ananias to this sin? Most probably the example of Barnabas, the wish not to be outdone by another. Alas! how much there is of asking what men will expect from us. The thought of the judgment of men is present to us more than the judgment of God. And we forget that our gifts are accounted of God, only by what the heart gives: it is the whole-hearted giver that meets Him. How much has the Church done to foster the worldly spirit that values gifts by what they are in men's sight, in forgetfulness of what they are to Him that searches the heart.

May the Holy Spirit teach us to make every gift part and parcel of a life of entire consecration to God. This cannot be till we be filled with the Spirit: this can be, for God will fill us with His Spirit.

4. There is still a lesson, no less needful, no less solemn than that of Ananias (Acts viii. 19). _The Holy Ghost rejecting Money._

"Simon offered them money, saying, 'Give me also this power.' But Peter said to him, 'Thy money perish with thee, because thou hast thought to obtain the gift of God with money.'" The attempt to gain power or influence in the Church of God by money brings perdition.

Here, more than with Ananias, it was simple ignorance of the spiritual and unworldly character of the Kingdom of Christ. How little Simon understood the men he dealt with. They needed money, they could well use it for themselves and for others. But the Holy Spirit, with the powers and treasures of the unseen world, had taken such possession of them, and so filled them, that money was as nothing. Let it perish rather than have anything to say in God's Church. Let it perish rather than for one moment encourage the thought that the rich man can acquire a place or a power which a poor man has not.

Has the Church been faithful to this truth in her solemn protest against the claims of wealth? Alas! for the answer its history gives. There have been noble instances of true Apostolic succession in the maintenance of the superiority of the gift of God to every earthly consideration. But too often the rich have had an honor and an influence given them, apart from grace or godliness, which has surely grieved the Spirit and injured the Church.

The personal application is here again the matter of chief importance. Our nature has been so brought under the power of the spirit of this world, our fleshly mind, with its dispositions and habits of thought and feeling, is so subtle in its influence, that nothing can deliver us from the mighty spell that money exacts but a very full and abiding enjoyment of the Spirit's presence and working. To be entirely dead to all worldly ways of thinking, the Holy Spirit alone can give us. And He can only give it as He fills us with the very presence and power of the life of God.

Let us pray that we may have such a faith in the transcendent glory, in the absolute claim and sufficiency of the Holy Spirit as God's gift to the Church to be her strength and riches, that money may be ever kept under Christ's feet and under ours, recognizing its only worth to be for His heavenly ministry.

Blessed Lord Jesus! teach and keep us that, like Barnabas, we may lay our money all at Thy feet, and hold it all at Thy disposal. Teach and keep us that like Peter, we may rejoice in the poverty that teaches us to prove our trust in the power of Thy Spirit. Teach and keep us, lest, like Ananias, our profession of living entirely for Thee be belied, by our giving to Thee. Teach and keep us, lest, like Simon, we think that the gifts of God or power over men can be obtained by money.

Most blessed Spirit! fill us with Thyself; come and fill Thy Church with Thy living presence, and all our money shall be Thine alone.

☩☩☩

III. THE GRACE OF GOD AND MONEY

.$.

"For ye know the grace of our Lord Jesus Christ, that though he was rich, yet for your sakes he became poor, that ye through his poverty might be rich."--_II. Corinthians_, 8:9.

In this and the following chapters we have Paul's teaching on the subject of Christian giving. In connection with a collection he wishes the Corinthian Christians from among the Gentiles to make for their Jewish brethren, he opens up the heavenly worth of our earthly gifts, and unfolds principles which ought to animate us as we offer our money in God's service. He does this specially as he cites the example of the Macedonian Christians and their abounding liberality, and makes them for all time the witnesses to what God's grace can do in making the ingathering of money the occasion of the deepest joy, of the revelation of the true Christlikeness, and of abounding thanksgiving and glory to God. Let us gather up some of the principal lessons; they may help us to find the way by which our money can become increasingly a means and a proof of the progress of the heavenly life within us.

1. The Grace of God always teaches us to give.--viii. 1.

"We make known to you the grace of God which hath been given to the churches of Macedonia." In the course of the two chapters the word grace occurs eight times. Once of "the grace of our Lord Jesus Christ, who for our sakes became poor." Once of "the grace which God is able to make abound to us." The other six times of the special grace of giving.

We all think we know what the word means. It is not only used of the gracious disposition in God's heart toward us, but much more of that gracious disposition which God bestows and works in us. Grace is the force, the power, the energy of the Christian life, as it is wrought in us by the Holy Spirit. We all know the command to stand fast in grace, to grow in grace, to seek for more grace. We rejoice in the words, exceeding grace, grace abounding exceedingly, grace exceedingly abundant. We pray continually that God would increase and magnify His grace in us.

We know the law of the Christian life: that no grace can be truly known or increased, except by acting it out. Let us learn here that the use of our money for others is one of the ways in which grace can be expressed and strengthened. The reason is clear. Grace in God is His compassion on the unworthy. His grace is wondrously free. It is always giving, without regard to merit. God finds His life and His delight in giving. And when His grace enters the heart, it cannot change its nature: whether in God or man, grace loves and rejoices to give. And grace teaches a man to look upon this as the chief value of his money--the Godlike power of doing good, even at the cost of enriching others by impoverishing ourselves.

Let us learn the lessons. If we have God's grace in us it will show itself in giving. If we want new grace, we must exercise what we have in giving. And in all we give we ought to do it in the consciousness of the grace of God that works it in us.

2. The Grace of God teaches to give liberally.--v. 2.

"Their deep poverty abounded unto the riches of their liberality, for according to their power, yea, beyond their power, they gave of their own accord, beseeching us with much entreaty in regard of this grace."

What a sight! And what a proof of the power of grace! These newly converted Gentiles in Macedonia hear of the need of their Jewish brethren in Jerusalem--men unknown and despised--and at once are ready to share with them what they have. Of their own accord, they so give beyond their power, that Paul refuses to accept their gifts: with much entreaty they implore and persuade him to accept the gift. "Their deep poverty abounded unto the riches of their liberality."

It is remarkable how much more liberality there is among the poor than the rich. It is as if they do not hold so fast what they have: they more easily part with all; the deceitfulness of riches has not hardened them; they have learned to trust God for to-morrow. Their liberality is not indeed what men count such; their gifts are but small. Men say it does not cost them much to give all; they are so accustomed to have little. And yet the very fact of their giving it more easily is what makes it precious to God; it shows the childlike disposition that has not yet learned to accumulate and to hold fast. God's way in His kingdom of grace on earth is ever from below, upwards. "Not many wise and not many noble are called. God has chosen the weak and the base things." And even so He has chosen the poor in this world, as they give out of their deep poverty, to teach the rich what liberality is.

"_Far beyond their power_ gave they of their own accord,

beseeching us with much entreaty that we would receive the gift." If this spirit were to pervade our churches and men of moderate means and of large possessions were to combine with the poor in their standard of giving, and the Macedonian example became the law of Christian liberality, what means would not flow in for the service of the kingdom.

3. The Grace of God teaches to give joyfully.

"The abundance of their joy abounded unto the riches of their liberality." (v. 2.) In the Christian life joy is the index of health and whole-heartedness. It is not an experience for times and seasons: it is the abiding proof of the presence and enjoyment of the Saviour's love. No less than our spiritual exercises, it is meant to pervade our daily duties and our times of trial: "a joy that no man taketh from you." And so it inspires our giving, making the offering of our money a sacrifice of joy and thanksgiving. And as we give joyfully, it becomes itself a new fountain of joy to us, as a participation in the joy of Him who said "It is more blessed to give than to receive."

The blessedness of giving: would that men believed how sure this way to unceasing joy is, to be ever giving as God lives to give. Of the day when Israel brought its gifts for the temple, it is said "then the people rejoiced, because with a perfect heart they offered willingly to the Lord; and David the King also rejoiced with great joy." That is a joy we may carry with us through life and through each day, unceasingly dispensing our gifts of money, our lives or service all around. God has implanted the instinct of happiness deep in every creature; it cannot help being drawn to what gives happiness. Let us get our hearts filled with the faith of the joy of giving: that joy will make to rich and poor our calls to give among our most precious privileges; it will be true of us, "and the abundance of their joy abounded to the riches of their liberality."

4. The Grace of God makes our giving part of our surrender to our Lord.

Paul says of their giving (v. 5), they not only did this, "but first they gave their own selves to the Lord." In this sentence we have one of the most beautiful expressions for what is needed to salvation, and what it is in which full salvation consists. A man who has given himself to the Lord: that comprises all our Lord asks of us; all the rest He will ndo. The expression is nowhere else found in Scripture; we owe it to this dealing with the matter of the collection. It tells us that giving money will have no value, except we first give ourselves; that all our giving must just be the renewal and carrying out of the first great act of self surrender; that each new gift of money may be a renewal of the blessedness of entire consecration.

It is only this thought that can lift our giving out of the ordinary level of Christian duty, and make it truly the manifestation and the strengthening of the grace of God in us. We are not under the law, but under grace. And yet so much of our giving, whether in the church plate, or on the subscription list, or on special occasions, is done as a matter of course, without aught of the direct relation to our Lord. A truly consecrated life is a life moment by moment in His love; it is this that will bring us to what appears so difficult, ever to give in the right spirit and as an act of worship. It is this will make "the abundance of our joy abound to the riches of our liberality."

5. The Grace of God makes our giving part of the Christlike life.--v.

"See that ye abound in this grace also, for ye know the grace of our Lord Jesus Christ, that though He was rich, yet for our sakes He became poor." Every branch and leaf and blossom of the mightiest oak derives its life from the same strong root that bears the stem. The life in the tiniest bud is the same as in the strongest branch. We are branches in Christ the Living Vine; the very life that lived and worked in Him. Of what consequence that we should know well what His life is, that we may intelligently and willingly yield to it. Here we have one of its deepest roots laid open; "Though he was rich, yet for your sakes he became poor, that ye through His poverty might become rich." To enrich and bless us, He impoverished Himself. That was why the widow's mite pleased Him so; her gift was of the same measure as His: "She cast in all she had." This is the life and grace that seeks to work in us; there is no other mould in which the Christ-life can be cast. "See that ye abound _in this grace_ also; for ye know _the grace_ of our Lord Jesus, that he became poor." How little did the Macedonian Christians know that they were, in their deep poverty, and in the riches of their liberality, giving beyond their power, just acting out what the Spirit and grace of Jesus was working in them. How little we would have expected that the simple gift of these poor people would become the text of such high and holy and heart-searching teaching. How much we need to pray that the Holy Spirit may so master our purses and our possessions, that the grace of our giving shall, in some truly recognizable degree, be the reflection of our Lord's. And how we need to bring our giving to the cross, and to seek Christ's death to the world and its possessions as the power for ours. So will we make others rich through our poverty, and our life be somewhat like St. Paul's: "poor, yet making many rich."

6. The Grace of God works in us not only the willing, but the doing. (v. 10.)

"You were the first to make a beginning a year ago, not only to do, but also to will. But now complete the doing also; that as there was the readiness to will, so there may be the performance also."

We all know what a gulf in the Christian life there often is between the willing and the doing. This prevails in the matter of giving, too. How many long for a time when they may be better off and able to give more. And meantime that wish, the fancied willingness to give more, deceives them, and is made to do duty for present liberality. How many who have the means, and intend doing something liberal, yet hesitate, and the large donation during life, or the legacy in the will, is never carried out. How many count themselves really liberal, because of what they _will_, while what they _do_, even up to their present means, is not what God would love to see. The message comes to all: "Now complete the doing also; that as the readiness to will, so the completion also, out of your ability."

"It is God which worketh in us to will and to do"; let us beware, in any sphere, of hindering Him by unbelief or disobedience, and resting in the _to will_, without going on to the _to do_. The Christian life needs exercise; it is by practice that godliness grows. If in anything we find that our giving has not been up to this Scripture model, not as liberal and joyful, not in as perfect accord with the spirit of our entire surrender to our Lord, or of His making himself poor for us, let us at once, in addition to the readiness to will, complete the doing also.

7. The Grace of God makes the gift acceptable according to what a man has._ (v. 12.)

"For if the readiness is there, it is acceptable according as a man hath, not according as he hath not." The God who seeth the heart, judges of each gift by the ability to give. And His blessed Spirit gives the upright heart the blessed consciousness that the gift on earth has found approval and acceptance in heaven. God has been careful in His Word to teach us this in every possible way. All the world's judgments of the value of gifts are reversed in heaven; the love that gives liberally according to what it hath is met by the Father's love from above. Let us seek to redeem our giving from all that is commonplace and little by taking hold of the blessed assurance: it is acceptable. Let us refuse to give what appears to satisfy us: let us pause, and rejoice in God's call to give, and in His Spirit that teaches how much and how to give, and the deepest joy of giving will come to us--the Spirit's seal that the Father is well pleased.

8. The Grace of God through the giving works out the true unity and equality of all saints. (v. 13.)

"I say not this, that others may be eased and ye distressed; but by equality, your abundance being a supply at this present time for their want, that their abundance may also become a supply to your want. That there may be equality. As it is written: He that gathered much, had nothing over: and he that gathered little had no lack." Another ray of heavenly light on this appeal for a collection. Money will become the bond of union that binds the Christians of Jerusalem and of Corinth into one. They are one as much as Israel was one people. As in their ingathering of the manna the feeble and the strong were to bring all into one store, that all might share alike, so in the body of Christ. God allows of riches and poverty, God bestows His gifts with apparently unequal hand, that our love may have the high privilege of restoring the equality. The want of some calls us to the love and the help and the blessedness of giving to others. And at another time, or in different spheres, the very ones who needed help may, in their turn, out of their abundance bless their helpers. Everything has been so ordered that love shall have room to work, and that there shall be opportunity to cultivate and to prove the Christlike spirit.

What a call and what a field in the needs of the world for all God's people to prove that God's plan is theirs: "that there may be equality," and that the spirit of selfish contentment with greater privilege has been banished by the Cross. In philanthropy and missions what a need for all saints doing their utmost "according to their power--yea, and beyond their power."

In sight of the heathen world, oh! what an appeal that there be equality and that we shall share and share alike with them what God gives us. What new, unthought of, eternal value, money gets as one of the powers for giving to the perishing, of the abundance we have in Christ.

There is no room left to enlarge on the further lessons of chap. 9. Let me just mention them:

(v. 6.) Let the giving be bountiful: it will bring a bountiful reward.

(v. 7.) Let the giving not be grudging or of necessity: the cheerful giver receives God's love.

(v. 8.) Let the giving be trustful: God will make all grace abound.

(v. 11-13.) Your giving brings glory to God by the thanksgiving of those you bless.

(v. 15.) Your giving reminds of God's giving, and calls to thanks for His unspeakable gift.

What a world of holy thought and heavenly light is opened up by the gifts of the Macedonians and Corinthian converts! Shall we not under the power of that thought and light review all our giving and see that it be brought into perfect accord with the Divine pattern in these chapters? Shall we not begin at once, and yield to Him, who became poor for us, everything that self-interest and self-indulgence has hitherto claimed and held? And shall we not beseech

Him to show in us by His Spirit that the one worth and blessedness of money is to spend it for our Lord, to bless our fellowmen, to use it as an instrument and an exercise of grace, and so to turn even it into the treasure that lasts for eternity?_

IV. THE POVERTY OF CHRIST

"Ye know the grace of our Lord Jesus Christ, that, though He was rich, yet for your sakes He became poor, that ye through His poverty might become rich." _II. Corinthians, 8, 9._

"THROUGH HIS POVERTY": what does that mean? That He dispossessed Himself of all heavenly and earthly possessions that the riches of earth and heaven might be ours? That He so took our place, as in our stead to walk in the path of earthly poverty, that we in comfort and ease might enjoy the heavenly riches He has won for us? Or has that "THROUGH HIS POVERTY" a deeper meaning, and does it imply that His poverty is the very path or passage that He opened up through which all must go who would fully enter into His riches? Does it mean that, just as He needed in poverty of spirit and body to die to the world that He might open for us the way to the heavenly treasures, so we need to walk in His footsteps, and can only through His poverty working in us, through fellowship with His poverty, come to the perfect enjoyment of the riches He came to bring? In other words, is the poverty of Jesus something for Him alone, or something in which His disciples are to share?

There is scarce a trait in the life and character of Christ in which we do not look to Him as an example--what are the lessons _His Holy Poverty_ has to teach? Is the right to possess and enjoy the riches of earth as it is now everywhere practiced in the Church part of what Christ has secured for us? Or, is it possible that the lack of faith in the beauty and blessedness of the poor life of Christ Jesus is part of the cause of our spiritual poverty; our lack of Christ's poverty the cause of our lack of His riches? Is there not a needs-be that we not only think of the one side, "For your sakes He became poor"; but as much of the other, "For His sake I suffer the loss of all things?"

In seeking an answer to these questions, we must first turn and gaze upon our blessed Lord, if maybe the Holy Spirit will unfold somewhat of the glory of this His blessed attribute. Unless our heart be fixed upon our Lord in patient and prayerful contemplation, and we wait for the Holy Spirit to give us His illumination, we may indeed have our thoughts about this Divine poverty, but we cannot really behold its glory, or have its power and blessing enter our life. May God give us understanding!

We must first of all see what the reason--the needs-be--was of the earthly poverty of Christ. He might have lived on earth possessed of riches, and dispensing them with wise and liberal hand. He might have come in the enjoyment of a moderate competency, just enough to keep Him from the dependence and homelessness which was His lot. In either case He might have taught His people of all ages such precious and much-needed lessons as to the right use of the things of this world.

What a sermon His life would have been on the far-reaching words: They that buy _as though they possessed not_. But no, there was a Divine necessity that His life must be one of entire poverty. In seeking for the explanation, we shall find two classes of reasons. There are those which have reference to us and His work for us as our Saviour. There are others which are more closely connected with His own personal life as man, and the work the Father wrought in Him, as He perfected Him through suffering.

Of the reasons referring to His work, the principal ones are easily named. Christ's poverty is part of His entire and deep humiliation, a proof of His perfect humility--_His willingness to descend_ to the very lowest depths of human misery, and to share to the full in all the consequences of sin. The poor have in all ages been despised, while the rich have been sought and honored: Christ came to be the despised and neglected of men in this, too.

Christ's poverty has ever been counted one of the proofs of His love. Love delights in giving, perfect love in giving all. The poverty of Christ is one of the expressions of that self-sacrificing love which held back nothing, and seeks to win us for itself by the most absolute self-abnegation on our behalf. Christ's poverty is His fitness for sympathizing and helping us in all the trials that come to us from our relation to this world and its goods. The majority of mankind has to struggle with poverty. The majority of God's saints have been a poor and afflicted people. The poverty of Christ has been to tens of thousands the assurance that He could feel for them; that, even as with Him, earthly need was to be the occasion for heavenly help, the school for a life of faith, and the experience of God's faithfulness the path to heavenly riches.

Christ's poverty is the weapon and the proof of His complete victory over the world. As our Redeemer, He proved by His poverty that His kingdom is not of this world, that as little as He feared its threats or its death could He be tempted to seek help from its wealth or strength.

But these reasons are more external and official; _the deeper spiritual significance_ of Christ's poverty will be disclosed as we regard it as part of His training as the Son of Man, and His exhibition of what the true life of man is to be.

Christ's poverty was part of that suffering through which He learned obedience and was perfected by God as our High Priest. To human nature poverty must ever be a trial. We were made to be kings and possessors of all things. To have nothing costs suffering.

Christ's human nature was not, as the Docetæ taught, a mere appearance or show. There never was one so really, so intensely, a man as Christ Jesus: "true man of true man." Poverty implies dependence on others; it means contempt and shame; it often brings want and suffering; it always lacks the means and power of earth. Our blessed Lord felt all this as man. And it was part of that suffering through which the Father worked out His will in His Son, and the Son proved His submission to the Father, and His absolute trust in Him.

Christ's poverty was part of His school of faith, in which He Himself first learned, and then taught men, that life is more than meat, and that man liveth "not by bread alone, but by every word that proceedeth out of the mouth of God." In His own life He had to prove that God and the riches of heaven can more than satisfy a man who has nothing on earth; that trust in God for the earthly life is not vain; that one only needs as much as it pleases God to give. In His person we have witness to the power which comes with the preaching of the Kingdom of Heaven when the Preacher Himself is the evidence of its sufficiency.

Christ's poverty was one of the marks of His entire separation from the world, the proof that He was of another world and another spirit. As it was with the fruit good for food and pleasant to the eye sin entered the world, so the great power of the world over men is in the cares and possessions and enjoyments of this life. Christ came to conquer the world and cast out its prince, to win the world back to God. He did so by refusing every temptation to accept its gifts or seek its aid. Of this protest against the worldly spirit, its self-pleasing and its trust in the visible, the poverty of Christ was one of the chief elements. He overcame the world first in the temptations by which its prince sought to ensnare Himself, then, and through that, in its power over us. The poverty of Christ was thus no mere accident or external circumstance. It was an essential element of His holy, perfect life; one great secret of His power to conquer and to save; His path to the Glory of God.

We want to know what our share in the poverty of Christ is to be, whether and how far we are to follow His example. Let us study what Christ taught His disciples. When he said to them, "Follow Me," "Come after Me, I will make you fishers of men," He called them to share with Him in His poor and homeless life, in His state of entire dependence upon the care of God and the kindness of men. He more than once used strong expressions about forsaking all, renouncing all, losing all. And that they understood His call so is manifest from their forsaking nets and customs, and saying, through Peter, "We have forsaken all and followed Thee."

The call of Christ to come after Him is often applied as if it were the call to repentance and salvation. This is by no means the case. The principles the call involves have their universal application; but, to expound and enforce them in truth, it is of great consequence first to understand the meaning of the call in its original intention. Christ separated for Himself a band of men who were to live with Him in closest fellowship, in entire conformity to His life, under his immediate training. These three conditions were indispensable for their receiving the Holy Spirit, for being true witnesses to Him and the life which He had lived and would impart to men. With them, as with Him, the surrender of all property and _the acceptance of a state of poverty_ was manifestly a condition and a means without which the full possession of the heavenly riches in such power as to convince men of their worth could not come.

With Paul the case appears to have been very little different. Without any express command we know of, the Spirit of his Master so possessed him, and made the eternal world so real and glorious to him, that its expulsive power made every thought of property or position disappear. He learned to give utterance, as no one else ever could do, to what must have been our Blessed Lord's inmost life in the words he uses of himself: "as poor, yet making many rich; as having nothing, yet possessing all things." And in his wonderful life, as in his writings, he proves what weight it gives to the testimony concerning eternal things when the witness can appeal to his own experience of the infinite satisfaction which the unseen riches can give. In Paul, as in Christ, poverty was the natural consequence of an all-consuming passion, and made him a channel through whom the Invisible Power could flow full and free.

The history of the church tells us a sad story of the increase of wealth and worldly power, and the proportionate loss of the heavenly gift with which she had been entrusted, and which could alone bless the nations. The contrast to the Apostolic state is set in the clearest light by a story that is told of one of the Popes. When Thomas Aquinas first visited Rome, and expressed his amazement at all the wealth he saw, the Pope said, "We can no longer say, 'Silver and gold have I none.'" "No, indeed;" was the answer, "nor can we say, 'What I have that give I thee. In the name of Jesus Christ of Nazareth rise up and walk.'" The earthly poverty and the heavenly power had been closely allied, with the one the other had gone. Through successive ages the conviction ever came that it was only by a return to poverty that the bonds of earth beneath would be broken and the blessing from above brought back. And many a vain attempt was made to secure to poverty a place in the preaching and practice of the church such as it had been in Pentecostal days. At times, the earnest efforts of holy men met with temporary success, soon to give way again to the terrible power of the great enemy--the world.

There were various reasons for this failure. One was that men understood not that in Christianity it is not an external act or state that can profit, but only the spirit that animates. The words of Christ were forgotten: "The Kingdom of God is within you;" and men _expected from poverty_ what only the Spirit of Christ, revealing itself in poverty, could accomplish. Men sought to make a law of it, to bind under its rules and gather into its brotherhoods, souls that had no inner calling or capacity for such imitation of Christ. The church sought to invest poverty with the mantle of a peculiar holiness, and by its doctrine of Counsels of Perfection to offer a reward for this higher perfection. She taught that, while what was commanded in the Gospel was the duty of all, there were certain acts or modes of living which were left to the choice of the disciple. They were not of binding obligation; to follow these counsels was more than simple obedience, a work of supererogation which therefore had special merit. Out of this grew the doctrine of the power the church has to dispense this surplus merit of the Saints to those who were lacking. And, in some cases, poverty became only a new source of self-righteousness, entering into covenant with wealth, and casting its dark and deadly shadow over those it promised to save.

At the time of the Reformation, poverty had become so desecrated as a part of the great system of evil it had to combat, that, in casting out those errors, it cast out a part of the truth with them. Since that time it is as if _our Protestant theology has never ventured to enquire_ what the place and the meaning and the power is which Christ and the Apostle really gave poverty in their teaching and practice. And even in our days, when God is still raising up not a few witnesses to the blessedness of giving up all to trust in Him, and of possessing nothing that one may possess Him the more fully, the church can hardly be said to have found the right expression for its faith in the spirit of Christ's poverty, as a power that is still to be counted as one of the gifts He bestows on some of its members. It will be found that there is no small difficulty in trying to formulate the teaching of Scripture so as to meet the views of Evangelical believers.

I have spoken above of the errors connected with the teaching of the Counsels of Perfection. And yet there was a measure of truth in that teaching, too. The error was to say that the highest conformity to Christ was not a matter of duty, but of option. Scripture says, "To him that knoweth to do good and doeth it not, to him it is sin." Wherever God's will is known, it _must_ be obeyed. The mistake would have been avoided if attention had been paid to the difference of knowledge or spiritual insight by which our apprehensions of duty are affected. There is a diversity of gift and capacity, of spiritual receptivity and growth, of calling and grace, which makes a difference, not in the obligation of each to seek the most complete inner conformity to Christ, but in the possibility of externally manifesting that conformity in such ways as were seen in Christ.

During the three years of His public career, Christ gave Himself and His whole time to direct work for God. He did not labor for His livelihood. He chose for Himself disciples who would follow Him in this, forsaking all for direct work in the service of the Kingdom.

For admission to this inner circle of His chosen ones, Christ demanded what He did not from those who only came seeking salvation. They were to share with Him in the work and the glory of the new Kingdom; they must share with Him in the poverty that owns nothing for this world.

From what has been said above it is clear that no law can be laid down. _It is not a question of law, but of liberty._ But we must understand that word "liberty" aright. Too often Christian liberty is spoken of as our freedom from too great restraint in sacrificing our own will, or the enjoyment of the world. Its real meaning is the very opposite. True love asks to be as free as possible from self and the world to bring its all to God. Instead of the question, How far am I, as a Christian, free still to do this or the other? the truly free spirit asks, How far am I free to follow Christ to the uttermost? Does the freedom with which Christ hath made us free really give us the liberty, in a love which longs for the closest possible likeness and union with Him--still to forsake all and follow Him? Among the gifts and calling he still dispenses to His church, will there not be some whom by His spirit He still draws in this particular, too, to bear and show forth His image?

Do we not need as much as when He and His apostles were upon earth, men and women to give concrete and practical evidence that the man who literally gives up all of earthly possession because he sets his heart upon the treasure in heaven, can count upon God to provide for the things of earth?

Is not this, amid the universal confession of worldliness in the church and the Christian life, just the protest that is needed against the so subtle but mighty claim that the world makes upon us? In connection with every church and mission and work of philanthropy the question is asked,

"_How is it_ that in Christian countries hundreds of millions are spent on luxuries, with scarce single millions for God's work?" Calculations are made as to what could be done if all Christians were only to be moderately liberal. I fear all such argument avails little. Help must come from a different direction. It was of the innermost circle that He had gathered around Himself that Christ asked a poverty as absolute as His own. It is in the innermost circle of God's children, among those who make the highest profession of insight into the riches of grace and their entire surrender to it, that we must find the witnesses that His Spirit can still inspire and strengthen to bear His poverty. He has done it, and is doing it. In many a missionary and Salvation Army officer, in many a humble unknown worker, _His Spirit is working out this trait_ of His blessed likeness. In the days we are looking for of deeper revival among God's children He will do it still more abundantly.

Blessed are all they who wait for Him, to receive His teaching, to know His mind, and show forth His holy likeness. It is as the first, the inner, circle proves the power of His presence, that the second and the third will feel the influence. Men of moderate means, who may feel no calling to the poor life, will come under the constraining power of the example and feel compelled to sacrifice far more of comfort and enjoyment in Christ's service than they ever did before. And the rich will have their attention attracted to the danger signals God has set along their path (Luke xviii. 25, Matt. vi. 19, 21, 1 Tim. vi. 9, 10, 16), and will, by these examples, if they may not themselves share in Christ's poverty, at least be helped to set their hearts more intensely upon the treasure in heaven--the being rich in faith, rich in good works, rich toward God--and to know themselves heirs of God, heirs of the riches of grace, and the riches of glory.

"That ye through His poverty might become rich." HIS POVERTY, not only as an object of our faith, but as a matter of experience and fellowship is the passage through which the fullest entrance is gained into his riches. Let us present together some of the aspects we have already pointed out of the blessedness Christ's poverty and its voluntary fellowship brings.

What an aid to the spiritual life! It helps to throw the soul on God and the unseen; to realize the absoluteness of His presence and care in the least things of daily life; and is to make trust in God the actual moving spring of every temporal as well as spiritual interest. And because it is not possible to claim God's interposition for every day's food if a man is not consciously walking in tender and full obedience, it links the soul to God's will and way by the closest of ties. The hourly needs of the body, which are so often our greatest hindrance, become wonderful helps in lifting our entire life into communion with God, and in bringing God down into everything. It elevates the spirit above the temporal, and teaches us in every state always to be content, always to rejoice and to praise.

What a protest against the spirit of this world. There is nothing the Christian life suffers more from than _the subtle and indescribable worldliness_ that comes from the cares or the possessions of this life. Through it the God of this world exercises his hidden but terrible power. This is the Delilah in whose lap the God-separated Nazarite becomes impotent and sleeps. To waken and shake out of this sleep more than preaching is needed, more than the ordinary Christian liberality, which quite comports with the full enjoyment of all that abundance can supply: there is needed the demonstration of the Spirit and of power, that God enables men, and makes it to them an indescribable blessedness, like their Lord, to give up everything of the earth that they may more fully possess, and prove, and proclaim, the sufficiency of the heavenly riches and the satisfaction they give.

The protest against the spirit of this world will become the mightiest proclamation of the kingdom of heaven, the self-evidencing revelation of how heaven can even now take possession.

What entrance it will give into the image and likeness of Jesus. We adore our Lord in the form of a servant, and worship Him in it as the most perfect possible manifestation of a Godlike Humility and Love. His poverty was _an integral and essential part_ of that form of a servant in which He dwelt. In all ages the love of some has given them no rest in the desire to attain the closest possible conformity to the blessed Lord. In Him the outer and inner were in such living harmony that the connection was not accidental; the one was the only perfect and fit expression of the other. In the body of Christ there are great diversities of gifts; the whole body is not eye, or ear, or tongue. So there are some who have the calling and gift to manifest this trait of His image, and for the sake of their brethren and the world, keep alive the memory of this too much neglected part of the ever blessed Incarnation. Blessed they whom His Holy Spirit makes the representatives of this His wondrous grace that, though He was rich, He became poor.

What a power then this poverty of Christ becomes to make others rich. It is through His poverty we become rich. _His poverty in His people brings the same blessing._ In the church, many who do not feel the calling, or who in God's providence are not allowed to follow their desire for it, will be stirred and strengthened by the sight. When some witness testifies to the blessedness of entire conformity, others who are not called to this path will feel urged, in the midst of the property they possess and retain, to seek for as near an approach in spirit as is allowed them. Christian giving will not only be more liberal in amount, but more liberal in spirit, in the readiness and cheerfulness in the forethought and the actual self-sacrifice by which it will be animated. Through their poverty, too, through Christ's poverty in them, many shall be made rich. Just as a specialist devotes himself to some limited branch of (say) medical science, and all profit by the exclusiveness of his researches, so through these, too, who love and live in and make manifest the poverty of our Lord, the church becomes all the richer. Through them the poverty of Christ gets a place in many hearts where it was not known, and it is seen how this was part of His overcoming the world, and how it may be a part of our victory that overcometh the world, even our faith.

I have said that all have not the same calling. How are we to know what our calling is? We may so easily allow ignorance or prejudice, self-indulgence or worldliness, human wisdom or unbelief to sway us, to keep us from the simplicity of the perfect heart, and to blind us to the full light of God's perfect will. Let us see where the position is in which perfect safety will be found, and where we may confidently count upon the Divine guidance and approval.

Not long ago I stood by the bedside of a dying servant of God, Rev. Geo. Ferguson, the principal of our Mission Institute. He told me how he had been meditating on a text that had come in the course of his preparation for his Mission class: "Though your sins be as scarlet, they shall be as white as snow." As he thought, it was as if one said to him, "_White as snow_, do you know what that is?" His answer was, "No, Lord, Thou only knowest, I do not." And then the question came, "_White as snow_, can you attain that?--can you make yourself that?" "No, Lord, I cannot; but Thou canst." And, again, he was asked, "Are you willing that I should do it?" "Yes, Lord, by Thy grace I am willing Thou shouldest do all Thou canst."

The three questions just suggest what our duty is. The heavenly poverty of Jesus Christ--do you know what it is? What it is in Him, in His disciples and in Paul, in His saints in later days? What it would be in you? Let the answer be, "No, Lord, Thou knowest." This is what we need first and most of all. If God were to open our eyes to see the spiritual glory of our Lord in His poverty, in _His entire renunciation_ of every thing of worldly comfort or self-pleasing; if we saw the Divine glory of which it is the expression; if we knew how infinitely beautiful it was to all the holy angels, how infinitely well-pleasing to the Father, we should then only in some little degree be able to say whether it was something we ought to desire and imitate. If we saw theheavenliness and the measure of the likeness to our Lord it would bring into our life, we should say, "I have spoken of what I knew not--Oh, that God would show me His glory in this too: '_for your sakes He became poor, that ye through His poverty might be rich_'!" Before you judge of it, pray by the Holy Spirit to know it.

Then comes the second question. "Can you attain it? Can you, in the likeness of Jesus, give up everything in the world for God and your fellowmen, and find your joy in the heavenly riches and the blessedness of dependence upon God alone?" "No, Lord, I cannot; but Thou canst work." Come and gaze upon the Son of God and worship as you think. It was God that made Him what He was, and that God can, by His mighty power, work in me His Divine likeness. Ask God to reveal by His Spirit, what the poverty of Jesus is, and then to work in you as much of it as you can bear. Be sure of this, _the deeper your entrance into His poverty_, the richer you are.

And if the last question comes to search the heart--"Are you willing for it?"--then, surely, your answer will be ready: "By Thy grace, I am!" You may see no way out of all the complications of your life. You may dread bringing upon yourself sacrifices and trials you could not bear. Be not afraid: you surely cannot fear giving yourself up to God's perfect love to work out His perfect will. For all He really means you to do He will most surely give light and strength. The Throne of

Riches and Honor and Glory to which the Lamb has been exalted is surely proof enough that there is no surer way for us to riches and honor than through His poverty. The soul that in simplicity yields to the leading of the Lord will find that the fellowship of His suffering brings even here the fellowship of His glory: "Though He was rich, yet for your sakes He became poor, that ye through His poverty might be rich."

✝✝✝